TRUTH FOR TRENDSETTERS

Affirmations of Faith for Those Responding to a Higher Call

Myrna R. Herndon

ISBN 978-1-64492-014-5 (paperback)
ISBN 978-1-64492-015-2 (digital)

Copyright © 2019 by Myrna R. Herndon

All rights reserved. No part of this publication may be reproduced, distributed, or transmitted in any form or by any means, including photocopying, recording, or other electronic or mechanical methods without the prior written permission of the publisher. For permission requests, solicit the publisher via the address below.

Christian Faith Publishing, Inc.
832 Park Avenue
Meadville, PA 16335
www.christianfaithpublishing.com

Printed in the United States of America

To my husband Astead who encourages and inspires. You've always championed me to go after my dreams and you are the best bible scholar I know! To my children Astar, Angelica and Astead Wesley and the greatest parents in the world, Gladys and Wesley Goodman.

52 Truths

I Am Not Alone 9
I Am What God Says I Am 11
I Think Rightly About God...13
I Give Up My Agenda 15
I Honor the Son..17
I Count My Blessings 19
I Look for My Escape Routes 21
I Have Usable Gifts and Talents..23
I Rejoice in the Lord 25
I Am a Leader Who Is a Follower 27
I Will Be Comforted in Sorrow 29
I Am Wonderfully Made 31
I Will Use My Sword Effectively...33
I Finish the Job...35
I Am Accepted 37
I Have the Power to Bless 39
I Will Receive a Reward..41
I Bring Forth Fruit 43
I Have Passion with Purpose...45
I Give My Best 47
I Can Accept No 49
I Can and Will Fight 51
I Come...53

I Have Peace 55
I Use Opportunities Wisely 57
I Carry My Cross Daily 59
I Reject Doubt 61
I Can Bring about Positive Change 63
I Am Lifted Through Praise 65
I Make Good Choices 67
I Patiently Wait for the Lord 69
I Need God 71
I Have a God-given Purpose 73
I Value Prayer 75
I Don't Despise the Moment 77
I Am a True Worshipper 79
I Look For His Return 81
I Have the Strength to Keep Going 83
I Know That Jesus Is Lord 85
I Have Power in My Spoken Word 87
I Overcome My Failures 89
I Believe in Miracles 91
I Am Prosperous 93
I Consciously Share My Faith 95
I Set Aside Time To Worship 97
I Have to Keep Knocking 99
I Need Forgiveness 101
I Am Blessed by Association 103
I Have a Teachable Spirit 105
I Don't Have to Help God Out 107
I Bury My Past 109
I Am Because God Is 111

PREFACE

There is a fundamental difference between facts and truth. Facts are something known to exist or to have happened. Truth is an actual state of a matter.[1] Daily we are confronted with a multiplicity of facts, some mundane others staggering. In any case, we must allow the truth of God's word to frame the facts of our lives. Being bold enough to allow truth to override facts will undoubtedly make you, regardless of age or profession, a trendsetter. The following 52 Christian truths as found in the Holy Bible, if embraced, confessed, cleaved to and proclaimed to others, will refresh and transform your life.

---
[1] Webster's Dictionary

Truth 1

I Am Not Alone

*God is always near, and I am an integral
member of the vast body of Christ.*

There are many great promises in the Scriptures. One of the most comforting is that God will never leave you nor forsake you (Deuteronomy 31:8). It is a trick of our adversary to make us feel isolated and alone. He is a liar. The last words of Christ as found in the gospel of St. Matthew are "lo, I am with you always, even unto the end of the world" (Matthew 28:20). Jesus was comforting his disciples then and us today with the promise that He will not abandon us. Not only is the Lord your constant companion, if you have confessed Jesus as Lord, you are a part of the worldwide body of Christ. You are of one mind and purpose with Christian believers who love the Lord Jesus and faithfully serve Him. At any given time, God can mobilize one of His servants to speak a word of encouragement that lifts your isolation and reminds you, God sees, and He knows. The Bible gives numerous examples of people who were used by God to bring hope fellow believers. Their testimonies are written to encourage us that regardless of where we are physically or emotionally, we can rest in the assurance that we are not without help (Romans 15:4). Become connected to a supportive faith community where you can develop

TRUTH FOR TRENDSETTERS

I will not fear what man shall do unto me the Lord is my helper!

meaningful relationships and know confidently that the Lord will be with you forever. He is true to His promises!

Scriptural Meditation
Hebrews 13:5-6 and Isaiah 41:10

Heb 13 v 5,6 — I will never leave you nor forsake thee

Truth Application
All week, encourage yourself verbally by thanking God for His presence. Find moments to encourage others who may be discouraged.

Ro 15:4 For whatsoever things were written aforetime were written for our learning that we through patience and comfort of the scriptures might have hope.

Is 41:10 Fear thou not for I am with thee ____ I will strengthen thee I will help thee I will uphold thee with the right hand of my righteousness

Truth 2

I Am What God Says I Am

I will speak what God declares about me rather than what others or I may say or think.

When you look at yourself, you will undoubtedly see flaws. Often these blemishes are barely noticeable to others. But sometimes, there are deeply embedded scars associated with troubling reminders of the past that you and others use to torpedo forward progress. Your imperfections or past mistakes do not have to hinder you from being used by God. Early in his life, Moses failed God and tried using his embarrassment as an excuse to reject his God-given assignment. God would not accept it (Exodus 3:11-15 & 4:1-17). God wanted Moses to see himself as God saw him. God saw Moses as a deliverer. Moses would only become that through the power and strength of God. It's not your own righteousness God desires. It is not a reliance on your own abilities and talents He wants. God seeks available people who are willing to lay all—strengths and weaknesses—at His feet and say, "Use me Lord for your glory." If you have repented from past sins and shortcomings, take your eyes off your weaknesses and put them on your God. His strength is made perfect in your weakness. Stop thinking and speaking negatively about yourself. You are what He says you are. You must think and act like it.

Scriptural Meditation

II Corinthians 12:9, Isaiah 64:6, Ephesians 4:29, II Corinthians 4:13, and Philippians 4:13

Truth Application

Select a biblical character that overcame personal failures to be used by God. Study their story and commit to heart and memory their transformational steps.

Truth 3

I Think Rightly About God

What I think about God is the foundation for all that I am.

The foundation of a building is critical to the safety of its structure. If the foundation is improperly laid, there is a good chance the building will not stand for long. The same is true about our spiritual foundation. The base of our spiritual life is our knowledge of Almighty God and His Son Jesus Christ who is the cornerstone of our spiritual house (Ephesians 2:20–22). What you know about God and how you correctly apply biblical teachings will make all the difference in your earthly existence. Jesus said anyone who refuses to apply His Word is like the person who builds their house on sand (Matthew 7:26–27). Only through study of the Holy Bible, prayer, and sound teaching can you gain an understanding of God the Father and Jesus Christ. You will also be able to *rightly divide* the word or correctly apply it (2 Timothy 2:15). The Holy Bible is the divinely inspired Word of God and study of the Scripture vital in understanding the nature and characteristics of God and His plan for humanity. He is omnipotent, omniscient, loving, true, just, merciful, and holy just to name a few of his divine attributes. What you think about Him is foundational to your spiritual development and outlook. Keep in mind, the deeper the foundation the taller the building. So think right about Him so your spiritual life isn't dwarfed, or even more disastrous, your spiritual house doesn't come crashing down.

Scriptural Meditation
 Matthew 7:24–27, Psalm 11:3, I Corinthians 3:10 and 15, and Isaiah 57:15

Truth Application
 Take several descriptions of God, like righteous or merciful, and study them. What do these attributes say about His nature? How did Christ exemplify them and what do these attributes say about Him being your God?

Truth 4

I Give Up My Agenda

I will surrender to God and allow Him to set the plans for my life.

The Apostle Paul's conversion was miraculous for many reasons. This great persecutor of the church became a mighty champion for the cause of Christ. And while the conversion of a soul, from darkness to light, is truly amazing, Paul's conversion was astonishing for another reason. This notable Pharisee of Jewish and Roman citizenry abandoned his rights and relinquished positional and spiritual authority unconditionally to God. Oh, how marvelous! On that Damascus road laid a broken Paul. Confronted with the reality of Jesus's majestic glory, a yielded Paul could only cry, "Lord, what would you have me to do?" (Acts 9:1–6). Such a remarkable and complete surrender usually does not occur without struggle. Yet in that extended moment, Paul reckoned that he must submit to the Lordship of Jesus and by doing so must allow Christ to hold the reins of his life. What a wonderful realization. Jeremiah 29:11 says, "I know the thoughts I think toward you, saith the Lord, thoughts of peace and not of evil to give you an expected end." God wants to set the course for your life. His plans for you are good designed with your good in mind. Give up your agenda and let Him have his way.

Scriptural Meditation
　　Psalms 25:5 and Psalms 139:23–24

Truth Application
　　Make a list of those things you're having difficulty surrendering. Pray about them daily that you will yield to God's will.

Truth 5

I Honor the Son

*I know who Jesus is and reverence his position as
the Christ, the only begotten Son of God.*

You believe in the Trinity—that God the Father, Jesus Christ, and the Holy Spirit are one. This may seem a contradiction to some, but it is the foundation of your Christian belief. There are many who may want to diminish the deity of the Son. They would like to say that Jesus was a prophet, a great teacher but no more. You must never diminish the role or position of Christ. He is God the Son who was with the Father from the beginning. And because God knows everything, he foreordained before the world that his Son would be given for humanity's redemption (St. John 3:13–18). The writer of Hebrews says that Jesus is higher than any created being. He is greater than the angels and most certainly greater than the devil and his dark forces. Jesus is the brightness of God's glory and the express image of His person (Hebrews 1:1–8). When we get to know Jesus, we know God, but you will never know God unless you honor Jesus as the one and only begotten Son of God.

Scriptural Meditation
    St. John 1:1–3, Philippians 2:5–11, St. John 5:20–27, and St. John 10:30

Truth Application

   Identify three characteristics or acts that distinguish Jesus from other prophets or great philosophers?

Truth 6

I Count My Blessings

I will be thankful for all God has blessed me with.

You are living in a world where many are simply dissatisfied and ungrateful. Sometimes it is a result of comparison. When you see what others have in light of your lack, it is easy to become discontent. Sometimes when your best efforts go unnoticed, disappointment can set in. Even more alarming, someone you deem undeserving is given recognition that rightfully belongs to you or another. Bitterness knocks at the door of your heart. It is nearly impossible to sustain an attitude of thanksgiving when dissatisfaction, ungratefulness, discontent, disappointment, and resentment fester within. You may be able to hide from others, but God knows the heart (Jeremiah 17:10). You must aggressively fight comparison with praise and thank God for what He has given you. Reject disappointment through prayer. Talk to the Lord about your hurts and injustices. Rise above the ungratefulness of our age by daily counting your blessing.

Scriptural Meditation
Deuteronomy 26:10–11, Psalms 61:2–5, and Psalms 103:1–6

Truth Application

If comparison has caused you to be ungrateful, pray for God's forgiveness and make a list of at least twenty blessings. Begin with simple things you may take for granted like sight, a place to sleep or clothing. Make sure your list includes spiritual blessings like a mind to live for Christ.

Truth 7

I Look for My Escape Routes

I rely on God to lead me away from temptations.

God is not counterproductive. He didn't die on the cross for you and then try to draw you away from Him. You are tempted when you are drawn away by your own lusts—the desires within you (James 1:13–14). You must learn to rely on God to lead you away from and out of temptation. Solomon was wise, Samson strong, King Saul anointed; but when they rejected God's counsel and leaned to their own understanding, they were no match for the devices of the enemy. The same can be said of Lot. When he leaned to his own understanding, he opened the door for the enemy. Drawn to the lush pastures of Sodom and Gomorrah, Lot dismissed these cities' wicked practices (Genesis 13). Moving his family to Sodom, he was in the wrong place when God pronounced destruction against these cities (Genesis 18:17–23). Lot's lineage proved no match against the seductiveness of Sodom. But because of Abraham's intercession, God was faithful to give Lot a way to escape. However, once outside of the city he failed to obey God's directions (Genesis 19:15-38). God will faithfully provide a way of escape but in order to be successful, we must listen, follow His directions completely and quickly take the escape route He provides. God will lead us away from temptation.

He is faithful, but you must be diligent to look for and take your escape routes.

Scriptural Meditation
I Corinthians 10:13 and Proverbs 3:5–6

Truth Application
List five areas of possible temptations and then identify methods to avoid them. If you are currently entangled in a situation that's displeasing to God, begin today looking for your escape routes. Ask a mature believer to pray with you. Accountability is a strong deterrent to temptation.

Truth 8

I Have Usable Gifts and Talents

I will utilize my gifts and talents for God's glory.

Like your natural body, the body of Christ consists of numerous parts or members. Some are visible like pastors and teachers. Those who enjoy the ministry of intercession or the gifts of helps may be less observable. The book of Acts records the formation of the New Testament Church. The Holy Spirit made use of the fivefold ministry (apostles, prophets, evangelists, pastors, and teachers) as well as gifts of healings, administration, giving, miracles, interpretation of tongues, and more (I Corinthians 12:28-31). It is the Lord who gives gifts to believers as He will. You may be unaware of what has been deposited within you, but you will grow in grace as you make yourself available to the church. Your giftedness will be revealed. Remember, never rush to validate a spiritual gift or covet the accolades of people. Seek to build up the kingdom of God and His church and be an encourager. The Bible admonishes you to esteem all who work in ministry (I Thessalonians 5:12–13). Make sure you don't just honor the visible members but seek out those less obvious. In so doing, you will learn about ministries that may interest you. You have usable gifts and talents. Search out how to utilize them for the glory of God.

Scriptural Meditation

I Corinthians 12:14–25, Romans 12:4–8, and Ephesians 4:11–12

Truth Application

If you're not currently active in a church or ministry, make yourself available as a volunteer or assistant. Identify at least two skills you possess or areas you would like to work in. Begin visualizing yourself at work in the ministry. Seek out ways you can utilize these talents immediately.

Truth 9

I Rejoice in the Lord

I am not ashamed to be demonstrative in my worship.

In Scripture, some of the Hebrew translations for the word *rejoice* are "to spin around," "jump for joy," "shout," or "be bright and cheerful" (Strong's Concise Concordance). Can you imagine jumping for joy or spinning around in worship? If you are a devoted sports fan, you have probably leaped for joy during the World Series, Super Bowl, or Stanley Cup. A skilled shopper has no doubt let out a shout when that bargain item was spotted and purchased. But the psalmist admonished Israel repeatedly to rejoice in the Lord (Psalms 33:1). This theme is carried throughout the New Testament as well with the church at Philippi being exhorted to rejoice in the Lord always (Philippians 4:4). Since the greatest commandment is to love the Lord with all your heart, soul, and mind, it is easy to see how believers can become demonstrative in worship (Matthew 22:36–38). Generally, whatever you love or highly regard, you will also become emotionally attached to. The next time you watch a sporting event and leap for joy or get excited about that spectacular purchase, ask yourself how often you have leaped or shouted for the Lord. And if you have not lifted up your voice in a shout of praise, ask yourself why not. Don't be ashamed to put yourself passionately into worship.

TRUTH FOR TRENDSETTERS

Scriptural Meditation
   Acts 3:1–10, Ephesians 5:19, I Thessalonians 5:16 and 18

Truth Application
   Select times and demonstratively praise the Lord in your home.

Truth 10

I Am a Leader Who Is a Follower

I will live my life so that others can follow me even as I follow Christ.

When Moses fled Egypt, the Lord led him to the tent of Jethro (Exodus 2:15–22). There, Moses found more than a wife. In Jethro, Moses secured a mentor who could instruct him in the manner of shepherding—a skill Moses would need as he cared for the children of Israel in the wilderness. After leading the nation of Israel out of Egypt, Moses the great leader would follow his father-in-law's advice in matters involving the handling of disputes within the camp (Exodus 18:13–24). After Paul's conversion, it was Barnabas who helped integrate the former Pharisee and persecutor into the community of believers. Barnabas was renown in the early church as a spiritual father (Acts 9:26–28). Through him, Paul learned the principle of discipleship and would later proclaim to others to follow him as he followed Christ. There is a pattern at work here. God develops leaders who are also followers. The humility acquired through following, the Lord wants emulated in your leadership. You will then become a leader who in turn mentors others to follow.

Scriptural Meditation

I Corinthians 11:1, Exodus 2 and 18, II Timothy 2:2, and Philippians 4:9

Truth Application

Make a conscious effort to mentor someone younger than you in the way of the Lord. Open communication and make yourself available to them. Your role is not to criticize them but encourage their development.

Truth 11

I Will Be Comforted in Sorrow

I will allow God to comfort me in my despair.

You have probably experienced grief and sorrow. Whether a close friend or family member has died or is suffering from a debilitating disease. Perhaps your family is in the midst of a terrible divorce, or you have lost all in a devastating natural disaster. Misery and heartache are part of our human experience. Jesus's close friends Mary and Martha suffered the loss of their brother Lazarus. His death was not only grievous but unsettling. They believed if Jesus had come immediately when called four days earlier, Lazarus would not have died (St. John 11:17–25). How often are you troubled by the thought that Jesus let you down? In times of despair, are you distraught asking, why God? Thankfully, Mary and Martha ran to Jesus during their time of grief versus running away from him. By doing so, He was able to comfort them and give a word of hope. During times of grief, tragedy, and pain, don't run away from the Lord or His church. He is acquainted with sorrow and grief and knows how to comfort us in loss, sickness, adversity, catastrophe, and anguish. Run to Jesus and stay in His loving arms. Allow Him to comfort you in sorrow.

TRUTH FOR TRENDSETTERS

Scriptural Meditation

II Corinthians 1:3–4, Matthew 5:4, St. John 11, and Isaiah 53:3

Truth Application

In times of sorrow or grief, find someone to pray with you. Having a person support you is critical. Don't isolate yourself from church fellowship and loving people. If you know someone grieving, send an encouraging card, invite them to breakfast, extend yourself to them, and pray for them.

Truth 12

I Am Wonderfully Made

I am a part of God's creation that He has declared was good!

God takes pleasure in his creation. After all, He made everything. Every variety of the animal kingdom, the intricacies of minerals, the expansive celestial bodies, the seas and vegetation, each insects, and the grand climax of it all—the human body—were formed by God the Creator (Genesis 1). Take a moment to fully appreciate the awesomeness of creation. God did and declared after the end of each creation that it was good. Advertising and entertainment are continually propagating their concepts of beauty. You must remind yourself that you are a unique design by the Master Creator. Whether or not you fit Madison Avenue or Hollywood's standards, encourage yourself that you are a reflection of His image and likeness. Regardless of your individual features, you are beautiful. Society's definition of beauty pales in the face of God's designs. Do not take for granted any aspect of God's creation. When you see a sunrise, proclaim that it is a testimony of God's great faithfulness. Marvel at the beauty of a butterfly. Praise God that you are a wonderful part of his awesome creation. Celebrate you!

Scriptural Meditation
    Psalms 104:33–34, St. John 7:24, and Psalms 139:14

Truth Application
    Remind yourself daily that you are God's creation—fearfully and wonderfully made. Don't accept societal standards of physical beauty as the only criteria for attractiveness but focus on your inner and spiritual qualities. The fruit of the spirit and holiness will make you beautiful.

Truth 13

I Will Use My Sword Effectively

I will study God's Word.

You may not know this, but you are in a fight. The Bible tells us that our fight is not with any human (Ephesians 6:12). It is a spiritual fight that demands spiritual weapons. The good news is that the Lord does not want you ill-equipped and has given you everything necessary for defeating your foe. One essential piece of your arsenal is used both offensively and defensively. It is the sword. Used to deliver a death blow or block the strike of your adversary, the sword is a powerful tool. In spiritual warfare, the Word of God is your sword (Ephesians 6:17). You must be skillful in wielding it to beat back your enemy. Jesus, when confronted by the devil in the wilderness, quoted the Word of God, not his own opinion to block the fiery darts of the wicked one (Matthew 4:1–7). The more you study the Bible and apply it to your daily life, the more successful you will be in your spiritual battles. Be a diligent student of God's Word. Read it daily and learn to employ it effectively because everything is subject to the authority of God's word. When you are called to the front line of battle, you want to be effective. Master the sword of the spirit.

Scriptural Meditation

Ephesians 6:10–17, II Timothy 2:15, Hebrews 4:12, and Hebrews 5:12

Truth Application

Become an active member of a corporate Bible study or Sunday school. Read the Bible daily and set goals to memorize scripture.

Truth 14

I Finish the Job

God enables me to start assignments but more important, He strengthens me to finish.

When Jesus was arrested and falsely accused, his disciples scattered in fear. It was a frightening and confusing time for those who understood Him to be the Messiah. Their King was crucified before He had the opportunity to establish his earthly reign. The community of believers was in disarray. Despite the confusion, several women determined that they would continue their ministry. Because of the Sabbath, Jesus's body had not been properly dressed for burial. Instead of abandoning the task for fear of persecution or even death, they pressed forward. God rewarded their faithfulness. They were the first to see the risen Savior (Mark 16:1–8). When God assigns you a job or births an idea, it is not uncommon for there to be obstacles. You must continually receive strength from the Lord to push beyond the fears and hindrances. Since the joy of the Lord is your strength, rejoicing in the assignment when challenges arise is one of the best ways to revive yourself (Nehemiah 8:10). God wants you to finish the work He assigns. There is no glory in starting an undertaking and leaving it half done. When Jesus died on the cross, He declared triumphantly, "It is finished." He completed the charge God assigned him. You too can finish the job!

Scriptural Meditation

Hebrews 12:2, II Timothy 4:7–8, Philippians 1:6, and Proverbs 20:4

Truth Application

List some things you've started and not completed. Go back to one or two and develop a realistic plan on how you will finish the job. Praise God for a new beginning and whenever challenges arise, begin to rejoice in the Lord.

Truth 15

I Am Accepted

*I will conduct myself as an heir of God
and a joint heir with Christ.*

If you have come to know Christ and are not of Jewish descent, then the New Testament refers to you as a Gentile. Take no offense; Gentiles who have been reconciled to God through Christ have been adopted into the family of God. But as many adopted children well understand, being taken into a family doesn't automatically make you a full heir of that inheritance. You must be accepted and awarded the same rights and privileges of the birth children. Scripture tells us that not only have we been adopted into the family of God, but we also have been accepted. You can cry Abba, Father. You are an heir of God and a joint her with Christ (Ephesians 1:3–6). You are a beneficiary of His promises. Be firmly planted in the knowledge that God loves you and as a result, He has accepted you. Conduct yourself as one who is a recipient of God's goodness and unmerited favor. You are a child of God.

Scriptural Meditation
   Ephesians 1:3–12, Galatians 4:1–7, Ephesians 2:11–17, Romans 8:14–17, and St. John 1:12

Truth Application

Search for Scriptures on the love of God. Commit them to memory. Remind yourself daily that you are not only adopted into the family of God but have been accepted. Conduct yourself as a joint heir with Christ.

Truth 16

I Have the Power to Bless

God has given me the ability to bestow kindness and thanksgiving. I will value it.

The Apostle Paul told the saints in Rome to bless those that persecute them, bless and curse not (Romans 12:14). This instruction was coming from a man who suffered maltreatment from both believers and nonbelievers alike. But the Apostle Paul had come to realize that the hallmark of a Christian is their Christlike nature. And that remains true today. You are to be like Jesus in what you do and say. If left to yourselves, you would not be able to achieve this. But thankfully, if we allow the Holy Spirit, He will empower us to have control even over what we say. Your tongue is a powerful instrument God wants to control (James 3:2). He wants to use your words to bestow kindness and thanksgiving. In His Sermon on the Mount, Jesus pronounced blessings upon those who would follow him. He cradled children in his arms and blessed them (Mark 10:13–16). Even to our enemy, Jesus said bless them (Matthew 5:44). God did not call you to curse, speak harm or ill will. Jesus often responded, "Be of good cheer" to those he encountered. As his disciples, you're to be a dispenser of good cheer. Be thankful for your food and life. Use your words to express your joy. Cradle a child in your arms and speak encouragement into their life. Enrich the lives of those around you. As Paul said to Timothy, be an example of the believer in both your word and conversation (I Timothy 4:12). Determine to speak blessings to those around you.

Scriptural Meditation
James 3:1–13, Romans 12:10–21, and Proverbs 6:2

Truth Application
There are people around you who have been damaged by words, determine that you will encourage them and use the Word of God to speak life.

Truth 17

I Will Receive a Reward

There are many blessings in this life, but I am anticipating my heavenly reward.

Olympians have medal ceremonies for their champions. Actors take home Oscars for exceptional performances. Top employees are given bonuses for exceeding expectations. Hardworking students are admitted to honor societies. Appreciation for excellence can bring a sense of joy and satisfaction to a student, employee, athlete, or artist. God rewards too, although his rewards are not for a talented few. When He lovingly showers creation daily with heavenly treasures like strength, mercy, healing, hope, and grace, God is pouring out spiritual blessings. In recognition of His faithfulness, these valuables are given by a just God who reigns over all of humanity. For those who obediently accept the Lord's salvation, they will receive the greatest reward: eternal life (I John 5:13). And will be a participant in the ultimate honors ceremony in heaven. The Bible says our heavenly rewards are so awe-inspiring, it's hard to fathom the good things God has prepared (I Corinthians 2:9). Your choice to be obedient to His word, share the good news with others, and perform good works will not go unnoticed. You will receive a reward.

Scriptural Meditation

Hebrews 11:6, and Ephesians 1:3, I Corinthians 15:58, Hebrews 6:10, and Matthew 25

Truth Application

Allow yourself to meditate on heaven. What will God say to you when He sees you?

Truth 18

I Bring Forth Fruit

*God expects the fruit of the spirit to
grow and abound in my life.*

The Bible relates a story that Jesus was journeying near Jerusalem and being hungry, came to a fig tree to eat its fruit. Although it was the season for figs and the tree was lush, upon close inspection it was found to be fruitless. Jesus cursed it (Mark 11:12–14). Hypocrisy on any level would not be tolerated. As believers, you are to possess the fruit of the spirit. These traits are proof that you are who you say you are. Without them, you are no more than a hypocrite. That's a strong indictment, but biblically true. God has so much faith in Himself; He guarantees that if you obey His word, you will become as a tree planted by the rivers of water that brings forth fruit in your season (Psalms 1). You're not to be like the tree Jesus encountered, appearing to possess one thing but lacking the fruit to prove it. There are many hungry souls that you will encounter. When they come, be prepared to feed them. Only if you bring forth good fruit will they be able to dine sufficiently.

Scriptural Meditation
    Luke 6:43–45, Matthew 7:15–20, Luke 13:6–9, and Galatians 5:22–25

Truth Application

Review the fruits of the spirit as found in Galatians chapter 5. What personality traits do you have that do not conform to God's character? List them and pray that God will help you become more fruitful in these areas.

Truth 19

I Have Passion with Purpose

*The zeal of the Lord will excite me but
also focus me in the right direction.*

There are times when enthusiasm about something reaches such a high point, you feel like exploding. You're ready to do something, anything to channel that elation. The same can be said about experiencing God. When you learn something fresh from His word or come to a revelation about the Lord, it will yield the same delight. You need a channel for your passion. The Prophet Isaiah saw the Lord. God was so majestic and awesome the posts of the temple doors shook with His voice. The experience left the Prophet wanting to work in the service of the Lord. But between the initial experience and the actual going, Isaiah was tempered with the reality of his own "nothingness." The brilliance of God's glory exposed all of his faults and blemishes. "Woe is me," Isaiah cried (Isaiah 6:1–8). Fortunately, God did not leave him despondent but consecrated and directed him. Neither self-pity nor aimless passion is acceptable. When you've had an awesome experience with God and feel like jumping over a wall and leaping over a fence, enjoy the moment but realize it's not about you. Direct your attention back to God. He will give balance and direction. Lord, how do you want to use me now that I've experienced you so dynamically? Have passion with purpose.

Scriptural Meditation

I Corinthians 9:25–27, II Corinthians 3:5, and II Corinthians 5:13

Truth Application

List three things that excite you and pray to the Lord to quicken a ministerial outlet that will allow you to utilize your passion for him. If you have purpose without passion, seek the Lord in prayer for a new fire and fresh joy. Remember, purpose without passion is drudgery.

Truth 20

I Give My Best

*I want excellence to be associated with
whatever I do for the Lord.*

Offerings are gifts and contributions that you willing give to the Lord. While offerings include financial donations, monetary gifts are only one aspect of biblical giving. You can and should present to the Lord your skills, time, and most importantly your life. Whatever you give, God wants you to put forth your best effort. Cain and Abel were brothers who both brought offerings to the Lord. Cain, who was a tiller of the ground, brought fruit of the ground as an offering. Abel, who was a keeper of the sheep, brought the firstling of his flock and the fat of his flock. It was the best and most well-nourished he had. God was pleased with Abel's offering as a result (Genesis 4:1–7). Sometimes we make the mistake of giving our best to everything and everyone but God. Or we're a wonder at church, but are subpar employees, husbands, wives, students, or children. If you're mowing the lawn, assisting a coworker, cleaning your room, coordinating a project, writing a poem, playing an instrument, helping out at church, studying your Bible, or babysitting your siblings, you please God by doing your best. Let excellence be associated with your character not in a selfish way, but as praise to God. It was the Lord who blessed you with your job, skills, life, family; determine to be a good steward over all that He has given and offer your absolute best at all times.

Scriptural Meditation

Hebrews 11:4, Colossians 3:17, 23–24, Ecclesiastes 9:10, and Daniel 6:1–3

Truth Application

The next time you finish a task, whether great or small, check your focus, energy, and attitude to see if you've done a job pleasing to the Lord.

Truth 21

I Can Accept No

*I realize the blessing of obedience and accept
the knowledge that God's no's are good.*

We crave independence. As children, growth is measured by our ability to walk unassisted, feed ourselves, and reason and rationalize independent of others. As a result, *no* can seem restrictive and take on a negative connotation. Hopefully, maturity teaches us that no isn't always bad but can be constructive and protective. The same can be said spiritually. Because we've yielded our lives to Christ and given Him the authority to direct us, when the Spirit tells us *no*, we can rejoice in that His foreknowledge is constructive and for our well-being. The Apostle Paul wanted to preach in Asia, but the Spirit would not allow him (Acts 16:6–7). The Lord wanted Paul to go to Macedonia. Although Paul's motives were pure, the Spirit knew what was best for him ahead and what would have the greatest impact. Not that he would have it easy in Macedonia, but Paul's blessing was in obedience to the Spirit rather than moving ahead with his own plan. Even when your plans are already in motion or seem perfect, if God issues you a *no*, stop! Rest in the knowledge that God is all knowing, and your delay does not mean forever denied. Accept *no* with the knowledge that all God's *no's* are good.

Scriptural Meditation
 Acts 16:6–40, Matthew 26:38–46, and II Corinthians 12:7–10

Truth Application
 Reflect on a situation or answer from the Lord that in looking at all the angles actually was for the better even though you were told no. Rather than focusing only on the "thou shalt not" of the Bible, read over the blessings of obedience found in Deuteronomy 28:1–13.

TRUTH 22

I CAN AND WILL FIGHT

*I am a skilled soldier understanding
the power of spiritual warfare.*

As a Christian, you may not want to think of yourself as a fighter. But the Scriptures clearly declare that you are in a fight and have been given everything you need to be victorious. Jesus spoke first of this warfare when he warned his disciples of persecutions that would come. "Ye shall be hated of all men for my name's sake…think not that I am come to send peace on earth: I came not to send peace, but a sword" (Matthew 10:22 and 34). Christians are followers of Christ. Therefore, His adversary, the devil, is now your enemy. The Apostle Peter said forasmuch as Christ has suffered in the flesh, we should arm ourselves likewise with the same mind (I Peter 4:1). Your victory starts with arming yourself with the knowledge that you are indeed in battle and as long as you fight the right way using the proper weaponry, your victory is guaranteed. And while our enemy may use flesh and blood, he is not. Therefore, our weapons must be spiritual and not natural. The Bible says that salvation, the Word of God, truth, righteousness, peace, faith, and prayer are our weapons (Ephesians 6:10–18). They may not seem powerful, but they are. In the midst of conflict, God uses them to humiliate the enemy, destroy his plans, bring glory and honor to kingdom of Christ. Understanding how to utilize your spiritual weapons when under attack makes you a skilled soldier in the Lord's army.

Scriptural Meditation
Ephesians 6:10–18, II Corinthians 10:3–6, I Timothy 6:12

Truth Application
Study each aspect of the gospel armor as found in Ephesians chapter 6. Purpose that you will be a skilled soldier.

Truth 23

I Come

I delight in knowing that God has invited me to come close to Him, therefore, I will come boldly to His throne.

Moses and Aaron, along with Aaron's sons Nadad and Abihu and seventy-nine of the elders went up to Sinai to commune with God after the children of Israel passed over the Red Sea. God had invited them to come up before Him. Since the beginning, God has graciously sought out humanity to commune with. This was true in the Garden of Eden as He looked for Adam in the cool of the day (Genesis 3:8). It is also true now. Jesus, who was God manifested in the flesh, invited children, those who were despised and rejected to come to him. His invitation contained a promise—that in coming He will give rest for the weary soul. We don't have to be shy or timid about coming to the Lord. The writer of Hebrews tells us to come boldly to the throne of grace, while the last chapter of the Bible closes with a plea by the Spirit to "come, and let him who hears say, come. Whosoever is thirsty, let him come." The invitation to commune with God is open. You should delight in knowing that the Creator of the universe, Almighty God, has invited you to come close to Him. Therefore, you should come quickly and boldly.

Scriptural Meditation

Exodus 24:1–18, Matthew 11:28, Isaiah 1:18, Hebrews 4:16, Revelation 22:17

Truth Application

Adam and Eve hid from God because of sin and broken fellowship with him. Examine your life. If you're not exercising your right to come close, it may be because of a broken fellowship. Repent for those things you know and wait before the Lord in prayer, so He can reveal more.

Truth 24

I Have Peace

The peace of God is nonnegotiable. I will not forfeit, lose, or devalue it.

There are perplexing scriptures that on the surface seem contradictory. One such scripture is found in Isaiah 48:22 in which God declares that there is no peace to the wicked. What seems perplexing is that outwardly at least, many that are ungodly seem happy and enjoying life to its fullest. And this may indeed be true. But peace is quite different than happiness. Peace begins with God. As Jehovah Shalom, He is the God of Peace. Peace emanates from Him as one of His divine attributes. Sin disconnects us from all that is godly. The Scriptures let us know when we accept Jesus Christ, we are reconciled back to the Father. We have peace with Him through Jesus Christ, and He in turns gives us His peace (Romans 5:1). It becomes part of our nature. We can and should live in peace, be peacemakers and seek peace. We must know that Satan is out to take this valuable blessing, and we should never forfeit it. Before Jesus's death, he promised his disciples an abiding peace to guide them through troubled times (St. John 14:27). In the midst of your turbulent seasons, don't give up your peace. Hold on to it knowing that it's a promise of God and an emblem of a true disciple.

Scriptural Meditation

Psalms 34:14 and 37:37, John 14 and 16:33, and Psalms 119:165

Truth Application

Take time to memorize a scriptural promise so when you are tempted to fret, worry, or be impatient, you can recite the Word of God to help restore your peace.

Truth 25

I Use Opportunities Wisely

I will take advantage of each moment and be prepared for what God sends my way.

As a Galilean who made pilgrimages to Jerusalem, Jesus most likely passed through Jericho. But on one occasion, his trip held more significance than previous times. On his way to Jerusalem to die for the sins of mankind, he would not physically pass through Jericho again. Zacchaeus may not have known this, but he seized his opportunity nonetheless and took advantage of the moment despite several obstacles in his way. Firstly, a multitude of people obstructed him from getting to Jesus. Crowds are often a hindrance to opportunities. Secondly, Zacchaeus was short in stature. Sometimes physical handicaps can impede your possibilities. And finally, he was "chief among the publicans, and he was rich" (Luke 19:1–6). Because publicans were known to cheat for monetary gain, Zacchaeus wasn't viewed kindly. A person's lack of character can also limit their options. Instead of giving up and forfeiting his opportunity, Zacchaeus ran ahead of the crowd and climbed up in a tree. Jesus noticed him and rewarded his effort. Zacchaeus not only received Jesus in his home but also in his heart. He made restitution to all he had cheated. Take advantage of each moment and be prepared for what God sends your way. This may be your only chance to utilize your opportunities wisely.

Scriptural Meditation

Ephesians 5:15–16, Colossians 4:5, Proverbs 12:24, and Luke 19:1–10

Truth Application

Think about the obstacles that have hindered you in the past—whether spiritual, physical, within or without. Take them before the Lord in prayer. Be willing to repent. Rethink how to regain an advantage and pray for windows of opportunities.

TRUTH 26

I CARRY MY CROSS DAILY

*I identify with Christ regardless of
where I am or what I'm doing.*

Death by crucifixion was commonly practiced in Jesus's day. In addition to being a painful agonizing torture, it was also humiliating. It was an execution primarily reserved for criminals. When Jesus began to instruct his disciples on how he would die, it's understandable why they reacted so negatively. Peter rebuked Jesus declaring it would not be (Mark 9:31–34). But Jesus had taught to his disciples that all who followed Him must identify with the cross (Luke 14:25–27). In fact, they must take up their cross daily. Apparently the disciples thought Jesus's lessons on the cross were merely symbolic. But being a disciple of Christ means demonstrating absolute loyalty even in the face of shame and suffering. On the road to Calvary, the Roman soldiers commanded an African named Simon to carry the cross for Jesus (Luke 23:26). Simon did not willfully carry the cross. He may have even been mocked for being associated with a criminal. He had to discount the embarrassment. It's not always easy to discount the shame that often comes with being associated Christ. Like Simon, it might be thrust upon you in awkward situations. Just know that the humiliation doesn't even compare to the glory that you will receive. When we identify with Christ, we're allowing Him to live through us. We're allowing Christ to be glorified. So take up your cross daily and identify with your Lord and Savior, Jesus Christ.

Scriptural Meditation
  Galatians 2:20, Matthew 10:38, and Romans 6:6–8

Truth Application
  Read the Gospel accounts of Jesus's death. When you feel pressured to deny Christ, take a moment to pray before you respond.

Truth 27

I Reject Doubt

*I may not understand what God is doing, but
I don't doubt He's able to do all things.*

God's ways are not your ways. His thoughts are above your own. There will be many times you will not understand how God is moving or what He's doing. That doesn't mean you can't seek to understand. In fact, you should. God doesn't want you lacking in wisdom or in the knowledge of Him. More important, He doesn't want you to distrust His ability. Doubt and unbelief are poisons that at best will slow your spiritual development and at its worst keep you from everlasting life. The Angel Gabriel appeared to both Mary and Zechariah. His message to both was astonishing. Zechariah's barren wife would have a child in her old age, and Mary, as a virgin, would conceive a son. Perplexed, Mary sought clarity to help her understand. Zechariah doubted that God was able (Luke 1:11–38). Even though God fulfilled His word, Zechariah had to endure unnecessary challenges as a result of his disbelief. It's best to be as the man who, when asked by Jesus did he believe, cried out for the Lord to help his unbelief (Mark 9:24). You should seek understanding but always fight the urge to doubt God's ability.

Scriptural Meditation
James 1:5–8, Hebrews 3:12–13, and Romans 4:18–22

Truth Application
Empower your faith by thanking God for all his incredible works. If you don't have any personal experiences, find biblical examples.

Truth 28

I Can Bring about Positive Change

I have the courage to speak out in love against injustices.

Queen Esther was in a position to bring about positive change. The problem was she didn't think she was able to do so. She initially lacked courage. When a plot to destroy the Jewish people was devised, Esther was asked to plead to the king on their behalf. Since the king did not know she was Jewish, Esther would have to put her own life and reputation on the line (Esther 4). There are times when the Spirit is tugging on your heart to protest an injustice. This can be a defining moment because your stance may separate you from the crowd. As Esther wrestled with possible consequences, her uncle admonished her with a compelling thought: maybe she was placed in the position as queen for this exact reason. Maybe this was her purpose for being queen. Esther knew she needed strength to do what was right, so she requested prayer and fasting, then she courageously went before the king. When the Spirit is tugging on your heart to challenge an inequity, examine yourself. Do you have the integrity to lead the fight or are you being appointed as a catalyst for another? Actively pray for strength and employ the prayers of other committed believers. God is concerned about those whose voices have been silenced by injustices. By employing the fruit of the Spirit, believers are able to speak out against injustices and bring about positive change.

Scriptural Meditation

Esther Chapter 4, Luke 4:18, Romans 12:21, Galatians 5:16–25, and Matthew 5:9

Truth Application

Embark on a joint study. Go through the gospel of Matthew and find examples of how and when Jesus spoke out against injustices and study the fruit of the spirit as found in Galatians 5:22–23 to learn more about Christian character.

Truth 29

I Am Lifted Through Praise

There are properties in praise that lift me when I'm discouraged.

There are so many reasons to be down. You lack financial stability. Maybe your family argues all the time. You may not have friends. You may be physically challenged. This world can be an unhappy place. But God gives us a prescription for depression and sadness, and it's called praise. The good news is, this prescription can be filled anywhere at any time. King David understood the potency of praise. During his years of exile, he experienced a range of emotional highs and lows. Praise became his remedy for equilibrium. At a place called Ziglag, everything he possessed was taken away. It was an agonizingly discouraging moment. Even his men considered stoning him. The Bible says in the midst of his despair, King David encouraged himself in the Lord (I Samuel 30:1–6). Loneliness, fear, anger, and doubt encroached upon him, but he used praise to combat the condition of despair. The joy of the Lord strengthens (Nehemiah 8:10). As a psalmist, King David used music and praise to build his inner most being. The Bible says that God has given you the oil of joy for mourning and the garment of praise for the spirit of heaviness (Isaiah 61:3). You must utilize these tools in the midst of despair. You will be lifted through praise.

Scriptural Meditation
　　Psalms 33:1–3, Psalms 34:1–3, and Ephesians 5:18–19

Truth Application
　　For one week, sing a song of praise every morning when you wake. Read the Psalms and create your own melody to one of the psalms.

Truth 30

I Make Good Choices

I will turn to the Word of God for instruction and allow the Spirit of God to direct me.

We are often confronted with issues and decisions that on the surface would appear the Bible doesn't address. You should understand that biblical truths are the keys to all aspects of life and when applied properly will bring you clarity and direction. The Apostles are a good example. Gentile converts were being birthed into the kingdom. This was a new phenomenon with major implications. Should Gentiles be required to keep Jewish laws? If so, which ones? As Jewish leaders, the Apostles could have leaned to their own understanding and traditions, but the results would have yielded spiritual death. Fortunately, they sought God in prayer, used the Scriptures as their guide, discussed the matter among Godly men of wisdom, and allowed the Spirit of God to speak to their hearts (Acts 15). Whenever you have a decision to make, let God's Word be your starting point, seek instruction from the Scriptures, pray, find godly counsel, and then allow the Spirit of God to speak to your heart. The process may be slow and deliberate, but you will find doing things God's way yields good success. You can make the good choices that give God glory and fulfill his master plan.

Scriptural Meditation

Acts 15:1–12, Joshua 1:8, Psalms 119:105, Proverbs 14:12, 15:22 and 16:3

Truth Application

Before making a decision, whether small or great, see what the Bible says about the issue, seek out godly counsel and pray for direction.

Truth 31

I Patiently Wait for the Lord

Since God's timing isn't my timing, I will wait on the Lord knowing that His time is the right time.

God, if you only would have been here. That was Martha's earnest declaration at Lazarus's tomb (John 11:21). She understood that Jesus had the ability to change things. But where was he when she needed him. Waiting on anyone or anything can be trying. Waiting on God isn't easy either. You can wait impatiently, angrily, bitterly, or in faith knowing that God knows and hears. How can this be done when the situation worsens, the deadline approaches, or there is none to encourage you? It can only be accomplished by meditating on the attributes of the only one who can help you. King David wrote, "Wait on the Lord: be of good courage, and he shall strengthen thine heart: wait, I say, on the Lord" (Psalm 27:14). Waiting in faith means waiting in full assurance that God hears your cry, and He will strengthen you as you wait. Remember, regardless of when He comes, it's not too late to change the situation for the good. During Martha's wait, her brother died. Jesus boldly declared to her, "I am the resurrection and the life; he that believeth in me though he were dead, yet shall he live" (John 11:25). In our wait, the situation can go from bad to worse to even loss. But Jesus's admonishment to

Martha encourages us that whenever He comes, all is well. Learn to wait patiently for the Lord. He will not let you down.

Scriptural Meditation

St. John 11:1–27, Isaiah 40:31, Psalms 40:1–4, 27:13–14, 62:5–8, James 1:3–4

Truth Application

Do a biblical search on Scriptures that speak to waiting on the Lord, looking up the meaning of *wait* and *patience* in the Greek and Hebrew. Commit several of these Scriptures to memory.

Truth 32

I Need God

I will commit all things to God's care. He is what I need.

Because we were created with freewill, we strive for independence by nature and celebrate freedom and individuality. So to declare a need for something or someone may seem limiting and juvenile in the natural. But God is neither something nor just anyone. He is Creator, the all-knowing, ever-present, all-powerful Lord of all who has revealed Himself to His creation. We cannot remove ourselves from Him. We exist in Him and because of Him. The Psalmist said, "If I ascend up into heaven, thou art there: if I make my bed in hell, behold, thou art there" (Psalm 139:8). We must bring our natural inclination for autonomy under God's sovereign authority consciously. Out of a willing heart, God wants us to recognize the privilege and honor of relationship with our Heavenly Father. We should delight in His presence and long to know Him more. When you come to understand that you need the Lord, in loving obedience you will commit all things to His care.

Scriptural Meditation
  Proverbs 3:5–7, Luke 12:29–31, Hebrews 4:16

TRUTH FOR TRENDSETTERS

Truth Application

Search the gospel of St. John for the seven "I Ams." List them and place beside each a personal, practical meaning.

Scripture: I am the good shepherd, St. John 10:14

Meaning: Jesus is the excellent shepherd who will watch over me, feed me, shelter me, and protect me from all hurt and predators.

Truth 33

I Have a God-given Purpose

*God has deposited within me divine purpose that
may be frustrated but will not be destroyed.*

You may not see all that God has placed in you or fully understand how He's directing your life. You're to busy living your life to give much thought to that. But if you are seeking to please the Lord, there are those who see His hand upon you and may seek to stop His purposes from being fulfilled. Joseph received through a dream God's divine blueprint for his life. Too young to comprehend the totality of God's plan, he believed in the Lord and lived a life that was pleasing to both his earthly and heavenly fathers. Joseph's brothers hated him because of his integrity and God-given dreams. They determined to destroy him. "Let us slay him and cast him into some pit…and we shall see what will become of his dreams" (Genesis 37:20). Sold into slavery and enduring years of hard cruelty, Joseph held on to the hope that God would fulfill His purpose. Dream slayers may envy or isolate you, try to make you break covenant with God, or seek to quiet you from sharing your godly aspirations but have hope. What God has deposited within you, He will protect. Maintain your integrity and be encouraged. Like Joseph, you have God-given purpose, and it will not be destroyed.

Scriptural Meditation
   Genesis 37:5–10, Genesis 39, Ezra 4:1–5, and Isaiah 54:17

Truth Application
   Write down all the things you desire to do that are God-inspired. Actively pray over the list. Ask the Lord to keep you from those who seek to hinder or destroy your purpose.

Truth 34

I Value Prayer

God has given me the right to commune with Him.
It is a priceless privilege I will take advantage of.

Christians know they should pray but often don't. For many reasons, this spiritual pleasure is too often neglected. Even as the disciples asked Jesus to teach them to pray, you must learn as well (Luke 11:1–4). Prayer does not come naturally. But the process of learning to pray is similar to a child who hears verbal expression, mimics it and ultimately begins to speak. We should place ourselves in environments where prayer is being rendered, pray ourselves, and then develop spiritual disciplines that deepen our communication with God. Then prayer becomes a daily necessity. The Old Testament Prophet Daniel could not live without prayer. As a high-ranking official in Babylon, he had come to rely on communicating with God three times a day. So when a law was passed prohibiting prayer to the True and Living God, Daniel disobeyed the law. When you make a conscious effort to talk with God, you develop a friendship with the Lord that will be as real and tangible as that of your natural friends. To have as a privilege the right to speak to God Almighty at any time is invaluable. You must learn to pray and take the steps necessary to value your communication with Him. Learn also not only to speak but how to hear His voice and understand His will.

Scriptural Meditation

Luke 18:1, I Thessalonians 5:17, I Timothy 2:1–3, Philippians 4:6, and Daniel 6:5–14

Truth Application

As you read over I Timothy 2:1 and Philippians 4:5, you will find that there are different types of prayer. Engage in a biblical study about the different types of prayer.

Truth 35

I Don't Despise the Moment

*I will enjoy the moments of my life
despite my age or circumstances.*

How many times have you heard someone wish they were younger or even older? When have you longed to be at a different point in your life? There's always a temptation to live outside of the moment. Instead of enjoying satisfaction today, we have a habit of longing for a better and somehow brighter tomorrow. But if we don't capture each and every moment, life has a way of passing us by. More important, we have a way of devaluing the grace and provision God supplies for today. Israel struggled with this concept. Daily, God provided manna for them in the wilderness. Yet their displeasure of the wilderness experience caused them to consistently overlook their daily miracles and ultimately forfeit their godly position (Numbers 21:5). In the New Testament, Timothy was a young man mentored by the Apostle Paul. Paul encouraged Timothy not to despise his age but live a fulfilled life in Christ by being an example of believers in what he said, in what he did, how he demonstrated love, and how he acted out his faith (I Timothy 4:12). Was that a tall order for a young person? Paul didn't think so. He had faith that as long as Timothy didn't despise his circumstances, God could do great things through his life. Don't live for tomorrow despising your circumstances or age. God can and will use you now. Seize the moment!

Scriptural Meditation
   Ecclesiastes 11:9, Hebrews 3, II Timothy 3:14 and 14 and 2:22

Truth Application
   Think about your life and the unique opportunities and skills you have at the age you are. What can you do today to make a difference?

Truth 36

I Am a True Worshipper

I worship the Lord in sincerity and truth.

Some people want to be applauded for believing in God. But Scripture teaches that demons believe and also tremble (James 2:19). Belief alone does not set you apart as a worshipper. That distinction is set aside for those who reverence God in sincerity and truth. The Book of Samuel tells us about two brothers who were from a priestly family, who held the right religious office but were not deemed true worshippers. They lacked admiration for and obedience to godly principles (I Samuel 2:12–17). Submitting to biblical doctrine qualifies you for worship but the responsibility to worship is yours. Because God is a Spirit, you can worship him anywhere. Because the Bible tells us He is seeking true worshippers, you should want to be found actively pursuing Him (St. John 4:24). The body of Christ is made up of people—like you—who have accepted Jesus as Lord and Savior and as a result of their belief, are openly expressing their love.

Focus your mind on God and his character. If you need to ask for forgiveness, do so. But wherever and whenever, lift up your heart and magnify Him. And as often as possible, open up your mouth and express your adoration to the True and Living God.

Scriptural Meditation
 St. John 4:19–24 and St. Luke 4:6–8

Truth Application
 Take ten minutes every day to worship God and then honor Him with your actions as well as your attitude and words.

Truth 37

I Look For His Return

Jesus is returning for His church and because I am a part of the body of Christ, I await with anticipation His return.

During Jesus's earthy ministry, he told a parable about ten virgins. Five he said were wise while the other five he dubbed foolish. The reason was apparent. While all of the virgins awaited the bridegroom's return, only five awaited his coming by keeping extra oil for their lamps. So when the bridegroom came at midnight, the five wise were fully prepared to meet him. Jesus concluded the parable with this warning, "Watch because you don't know the day or the hour the Son of Man will return" (Matthew 25:1–13). Jesus said He would come back for His church. Although we don't know the day or the hour, we should stay prepared to receive him. In the last chapter of Revelation Jesus says, "I am coming soon" and reiterates "Surely I come quickly." But the true joy of this revelation comes through the Apostle John by inspiration of the Holy Spirit. "Even so, come, Lord Jesus." Although his return may seem delayed, keep yourself renewed by the promise that He is coming back. Don't be like the five foolish virgins. Wait with anticipation and know without doubt that Jesus is returning for His church.

Scriptural Meditation

Matthew 25:1–13, St. John 14:1–3, Acts 1:11, I Thessalonians 4:13–18, and Revelation 22

Truth Application

Share with someone the biblical truth that Jesus is coming back for his church.

Truth 38

I Have the Strength to Keep Going

My march of faith may have some uphill climbs, but I purpose to keep moving.

How do you know you're doing what God desires? Do you have peace about it? Is the path before you clear? Christians everywhere want assurances of God's course for their lives. Don't make the mistake of thinking the quicker and easier path is more in line with His will. The Prophet Samuel anointed David King of Israel. As God's choice, you would think David's ascension to the throne would have been easy. Yet the road of obedience can have some dips, curves, and even bumps. It took years of challenges, disappointments, and spiritual battles before the fulfillment of God's promise in David's life (I Samuel 19:1–18). Don't think for a moment that ease and comfort are the sole indicators of God's presence and purpose. God promises that if our march of faith takes us through the shadow of death, He will be with us (Psalm 23). Your march may currently be an uphill battle, but God will strengthen you to keep going.

Scriptural Meditation
 I Samuel 16:1–13, I Samuel 18:1–14, I Samuel 19:1–18, and Galatians 6:9

Truth Application

List some goals that are currently being hindered or delayed. Then list the obstacles. Pray to the Lord to show you methods to resolve or remove them.

Truth 39

I Know That Jesus Is Lord

*In respect to His Lordship, I choose to
bow in reverence to Him now.*

The Apostle Paul said to the church at Corinth, "To us there is but one God, the Father, of whom are all things, and we in Him, and one Lord Jesus Christ, by whom are all things, and we by Him" (I Corinthians 8:6). In identifying Jesus as Lord, Paul was saying Christ is both the master and superior officer of our lives. This truth is the bedrock upon which the believer's faith rest. It was the obedient act of Christ, humbling himself unto death, which brought glory to God and rendered Satan powerless. The Scriptures tell us that for this reason, God has highly exalted Jesus and elevated His name above all names. As a result, everything in both heaven and earth will have to acknowledge the Lordship of Jesus Christ (Philippians 2:10 and 11). Accepting and reverencing Jesus as Lord is done so with your words and through your actions. Jesus said, "Why call me Lord, Lord and do not the things which I say?" (Luke 6:46). When you accept the Lordship of Christ, you're making a decision to walk in obedience to His word. This puts you in harmony with Almighty God. Agreement with God secures His grace, favor, peace, and every spiritual blessing. When you know that Jesus is Lord and make the decision to reverence Him as Lord, you are building your spiritual house upon a solid foundation.

Scriptural Meditation
   Philippians 2:2–11, Matthew 16:13–20, Hebrews 1:1–9, John 5:22 and 23, St. John 14:6, and Luke 6:46–49

Truth Application
   Determine that you will take a stand for Jesus when conversations about God and Christianity arise in your presence. Walk away celebrating your boldness to speak up regardless of the outcome.

Truth 40

I Have Power in My Spoken Word

Since God has given life and death in the power of the tongue, I will value this privilege.

The ability to speak is a powerful tool God gave to humanity. How often do you consider the power of your words? Do you rattle off endlessly or withhold your opportunity to speak faith? The Bible says that death and life are in the power of the tongue (Proverbs 18:21). The children of Israel during their wilderness experience used their tongues to create a negative environment of criticism rather than use the verbal authority God gave them to agree with His word (Exodus 16:2 and 12). Today, lying and using filthy language are fashionable, murmuring and complaining commonplace. Contrariwise, your speech should clearly identify you as a child of God, one who understands the value and privilege He has given through the spoken word. When Jesus was arrested, Peter's speech identified him as a follower of Christ. Out of fear, Peter began to curse and deny the Lord. When you curse and lie, you are grieving the Lord separating yourself from Him. When you speak the truth and edifying words, you please the Spirit ministering grace to the hearers (Ephesians 4:29 and 31). When you speak the word of God, faith is produced (Romans 10:17). Ultimately and perhaps more important, God has given you the ability to communicate with Him through your spoken word.

You cannot devalue this great privilege. When you talk to the Lord, speak plainly knowing it's not flowery words that impress but an honest and contrite heart.

Scriptural Meditation
　　Matthew 12:36–37, James 3:2–13, Philippians 2:14, and Colossians 4:6

Truth Application
　　Challenge yourself this week to watch what comes out of your mouth. Are you a reactive or proactive communicator? Do your words reflecting faith or doubt? Step up your communication with the Lord in prayer as well.

Truth 41

I Overcome My Failures

My mistakes will not forever cloud my future.

You've made mistakes. Everyone has. The issue for most of us is, how will we overcome our failures? Sarah was a beautiful woman who had a problem she did not create. She desperately wanted children but was unable to have them. Since God had promised she and Abraham a child, she decided the best way to fulfill God's promise was for her servant Hagar to give birth. Feeling despondent and hopeless, Sarah allowed her husband to conceive a child with Hagar (Genesis 16:1–6). It was a mistake. Even more devastating, it was a mistake that was forever before her. If your mistake is open before everyone, shame and embarrassment may well be associated with it. Sarah was openly humiliated when Hagar started treating her disrespectfully. What could she do? She tried to confront Hagar, which only intensified the problem. Sarah had to believe God. Trust and faith in the Lord and His Word will help you overcome your failures. When you've repented of your shortcomings, the Bible tells us God remembers them no more (Jeremiah 31:34). When we take hold of His Word, He will also heal us, build our esteem, and help us to forgive ourselves. By faith in God's Word, Sarah received strength to overcome her failures and conceive (Hebrews 11:11). Your future doesn't have to remain cloudy. You don't have to be bound by your mistakes. Take hold of God's Word and be healed.

Scriptural Meditation
Genesis 16:1–6, Genesis 21:5–21, Luke 22:54–62, St. John 21:15–19, and Psalm 103:12

Truth Application
Pray and ask the Lord's help in overcoming fear and shame associated with the mistakes you have made. By faith, speak affirmatively and anticipate positive things occurring in your near future.

Truth 42

I Believe in Miracles

Because God is able to do the miraculous, I will turn to him to work out my impossible situations.

Because so many prayers seem to go unanswered, there's a tendency to think God is not omnipotent or that His power and authority is somehow limited. However, there are some things you should know to be true about God regardless of what He does or does not do, because the Word of God declares it to be so. It's important that you consistently check yourself to make sure you still hold biblical truths as cornerstones of your faith. Two of these absolutes are: God cannot lie, and He is the same yesterday, today and forever (Titus 1:2 and Hebrews 13:8). The Bible is a testimony of God and His dealings with humanity. There are numerous wonders recorded from the parting of the Red Sea, and a donkey rebuking the false Prophet Balaam, to the miraculous birth of our Lord Jesus, and the healing shadow ministry of the Apostle Peter. If God was a miracle worker in ancient times, He still can work miracles today. Secular thinking should not invade your mind to believe otherwise. As long as you have breath, you must believe God, feel confident in talking to him about everything and believe He still works miracles. This will not narrow your thinking but broadens your possibilities all the while placing you as a candidate for the miraculous today.

Scriptural Meditation
Mark 11:24, Mark 9:14–29, Matthew 21: 18–22, and Hebrews 2:1–4

Truth Application
Whenever you are confronted with impossible situations, declare over all thoughts of doubts, "God, you are able to do all things. I still believe in miracles. Help that part of me that can't believe."

Truth 43

I Am Prosperous

As I walk in the way of righteousness and delight myself in the Lord, I will be prosperous.

There are two biblical references of Joseph being prosperous, and both of these declarations were made at unfavorable times in his life. The first came when his brothers sold him into slavery. The Bible says that the Lord was with him, and he was "a prosperous man" (Genesis 39:2). The second reference was when Joseph was taken to the King's prison under false accusations. The Bible states again that the Lord was with him and made him "to prosper" (Genesis 39:23). The first psalm gives the résumé of the person who delights and meditates in the law of the Lord. The resounding conclusion is whatever state this person finds themselves in, it will be prosperous. Biblical prosperity isn't validated by luxury, money, position or status but fostered by your relationship with the Lord and manifested through contented confidence in the God of the universe who said, "For every beast of the forest is mine, and the cattle upon a thousand hills" (Psalm 50:10). Stop seeking things to validate your prosperity. Conduct yourself with dignity and integrity. Seek God and when you obtain His righteousness, you will be the possessor of an abundant inheritance.

Scriptural Meditation
   Genesis 39:1–6, Genesis 39:11–23, Psalms 1, III John 2

Truth Application
   Pray for yourself the prayer Paul made for the church in Ephesus. "Cease not to give thanks for you, making mention of you in my prayers. That the God of our Lord Jesus Christ, the Father of glory, may give unto you the spirit of wisdom and revelation in the knowledge of him: The eyes of your understanding being enlightened, that ye may know what is the hope of his calling, and what the riches of the glory of his inheritance in the saints" (Ephesians 1:16–18). Pray it until your able to believe God that you are indeed walking in prosperity.

Truth 44

I Consciously Share My Faith

Fear nor other's opinions will not stop me from sharing my love and commitment for Christ.

Soul winning is often called an "art" because many believe effective soul winning requires forethought, strategy, and skill. The Bible bestows high praise on soul winners by saying the person who wins souls is wise (Proverbs 11:30). As a result, some become bogged down introspectively with the prospect of being foolish or ineffective in their attempt to witness. Being committed to sharing your faith should not generate fear or pressure. It should be an easy pleasure to talk about the One who has brought joy to your life, changing both your earthly perspective and eternal destination. When a person rejects Christ, it is not an indictment against you personally. Your commission is to share your faith not to save. It is the job of the Holy Spirit to convict and the Word to bring faith unto salvation. "The law of the Lord is perfect, converting the soul: the testimony of the Lord is sure, making wise the simple" (Psalm 19:7). Not everyone accepts Christ immediately. Paul, one of the greatest soul winners, wasn't successful every time. In fact philosophers and theologians consider his sermon on Mars Hill as one of the greatest yet it ended with few positive respondents. Don't veil what God has done or is doing. "Let your light so shine before men, that they may see your good works, and glorify your Father which is in heaven" (Matthew 5:16). Be deliberate about sharing the good news.

Scriptural Meditation
   Romans 1:16, Acts 17:16–34, and Luke 12:8–9, Romans 6:23

Truth Application
   Role-play with a friend situations or arguments people may use to reject Christ and come up with appropriate strategies. Remember that receiving Christ is as easy as ABC. *Accept* the authority of God's word and acknowledge a need for a savior. *Believe* the finished work at the cross and that Jesus is the Son of God. *Confess* that you have fallen short, repent, and commit your life to Jesus from that moment forward.

Truth 45

I Set Aside Time To Worship

*I will not rush my worship but bask in His
glory and linger in His presence.*

When the children of Israel left Egypt, they traveled through the desert for forty years. God gave them numerous commandments, laws, and ordinances covering a wide range of issues. Part of God's revelation to Moses on Mt. Sinai was regarding exactly how He wanted Israel to worship Him. They were to erect a large tent, called the tabernacle, where priests would offer sacrifices to God for themselves and for the people. The tabernacle, with its altar, candlesticks, bowls, lavers, and the like, had to be erected precisely. Since sacrificing required an unblemished animal, a thorough search had to be made (Exodus 23–29). In other words, worship took time. In fact, God commanded them to set aside an entire day for worship called the Sabbath. We are obviously living in a different era. Speed dial calls, microwave meals, self-checkout counters. The temptation is to also rush when it comes to worship. God speaks to us during those quiet times of meditation and prayer. Don't fall into the trap of trying to rush God. Cherish His presence. Set aside time for worship. Bask in His glory. "Thou wilt shew me the path of life: in thy presence is fulness of joy; at thy right hand there are pleasures for evermore" (Psalms 16:11). Learn to linger in His presence and not rush your worship.

Scriptural Meditation
    Exodus 20:8–11, Deuteronomy 5:12–15, Exodus 40

Truth Application
    Challenge yourself to a daily time of prayer and meditation on the Scriptures. Find a church where worship is a part of the experience and become a willing participant.

Truth 46

I Have to Keep Knocking

I understand that persistent prayer is a biblical principle.

How many athletes would be successful if they shot a basketball, swung at a baseball, or ran around a track just once? What student would ever graduate if they became disappointed after receiving one poor test grade or faced one difficult teacher? The concept of tenacious effort to achieve natural goals seems easier to accept then the thought of working hard to obtain our spiritual objectives. For some reason, many of us feel that one or two quick prayers, requests or thoughts toward a situation merits God's immediate attention. The Lord Jesus gave a parable to his disciples rousing them that persistence in prayer pays off (Luke 18:1–8). Jesus told them of an ungodly judge who refused to hear the petitions of a widow. But because this woman bombarded the judge repeatedly, eventually this judge granted her request just to send her away. Jesus said he gave this parable so that we would always pray and not lose heart when tempted to give up. If you want to receive from the Lord, confess your shortcomings and make sure you're abiding in Christ. Then come humbly but boldly to the throne of grace asking in faith. You just might have to ask and keep asking, seek and keep seeking, knock and keep knocking. There's nothing wrong with persistence in prayer, it's a biblical principle that commands attention.

Scriptural Meditation

Matthew 7:7–8, James 5:13–18, Proverbs 8:17, and I Kings 18:41–45

Truth Application

When you're engaged in a persistent prayer battle, make sure to begin and end each prayer with praise and thanksgiving. This will build you up spiritually.

Truth 47

I Need Forgiveness

I am not too proud to ask for or receive forgiveness.

Adam, the first created human, was formed perfect and righteous in the sight of God. But when he disobeyed God, he not only lost his holy state, but sin and death entered the world. Now we are all born into a sinful world and molded in immorality. Thankfully, God, through his mercy, provided a remedy for sin and its effects. He would come as God the Son and present himself as the perfect sacrifice. For God had already determined that without the shedding of blood there would be no remission of sins (Hebrews 9:22). Therefore, although in Adam all died spiritually, through the blood of Jesus all can be made alive (I Corinthians 15:21–22). Accepting God's plan of salvation from sin, death, and separation from God starts with our confession that Jesus is indeed God the Son who came so that we would have eternal life and be acceptable to the Father. Once you have made the confession of faith in Christ Jesus, you are a new creation. However, there are times you may fall short of doing God's will. At those times, remember you are in need of Christ's forgiving love too. Whenever you sin you have an advocate with the Father in Jesus Christ (I John 2:1). Go to Christ, confess your sins, and He is faithful to forgive and cleanse you. Don't be too proud or too ashamed to ask for and receive the forgiveness of God. In repentance, there is power to equip you with victorious strength over your areas of struggle and temptation.

Scriptural Meditation

Romans 5:17–21, St. John 3:16–18, I John 2:1–5, and I Corinthians 15:22

Truth Application

Be conscious of times you disappoint or grieve the Holy Spirit because of disobedience. Make sure you ask for forgiveness and immediately set a course that reflects obedience. Psalm 51 is a wonderful study on how King David sought God for forgiveness.

TRUTH 48

I Am Blessed by Association

Who I choose to associate with makes a difference.

Lot was faced with a choice. Separate himself from Abraham or try to work out the differences that caused their herdsmen to quarrel. Lot chose the former (Genesis 13:1–13). Looking up and seeing the green, fruitful plains of Jordan, he moved closer to Sodom despite two critical factors. The people of Sodom were wicked in God's sight thus moving closer to Sodom would require Lot to separate himself in order to maintain his righteous stand with God. Equally important, Lot's blessing came to him because of his association with Abraham. It would seem that staying with Abraham or seeking Abraham's advice would have made better sense. Moving closer to Sodom not only disconnected him from Abraham and his blessing but also adversely affected his family. Watch your associations. Make a conscious choice to be with godly people who will encourage and support you in your righteous walk. While all of us have to associate with unbelievers, when you have a choice, choose to be blessed by godly associations.

Scriptural Meditation
    Genesis 18 and 19, I Corinthians 15:33, II Thessalonians 3:6–9, and Amos 3:3

Truth Application

Evaluate your friendships and associations. Those that are not promoting and supporting your walk with God begin active prayer for God to replace these with more committed believers. Start replacing some of the time you spend with unbelievers by helping in the church with ministry activities. Look for a spiritual mentor as well.

Truth 49

I Have a Teachable Spirit

Regardless of how God uses me, I will remain humble.

Meekness is in no wise associated with weakness. Meekness encompasses humility and the ability to posses a teachable spirit. In the book of Acts, the Bible introduces us to friends of the Apostle Paul, a married couple named Priscilla and Aquila (Acts 18:1–2). This ministry duo encountered an Alexandrian Jew named Apollos while in Ephesus. He was described as "eloquent," "mighty" in the Scriptures, and "fervent in the spirit." Although he spoke boldly about the ministry of John the Baptist, Apollos lacked a full understanding of the gospel message. Thankfully this articulate, persuasive scholar possessed a teachable spirit. For when Priscilla and Aquila invited him to their house to explain to him the way of God more adequately, not only did he accept their invitation but also came to know Jesus Christ personally. Humility is the ingredient that allows the body of Christ to operate at its fullest capacity. Regardless of your gifts and talents, cultivate a teachable spirit. God has called us all to be subject to each other and "clothed with humility: for God resisteth the proud, and giveth grace to the humble" (I Peter 5:5).

Scriptural Meditation

Acts 18:24–28, Matthew 5:5, Psalms 147:6 and 149:4, II Timothy 2:24–25, James 1:21, Philippians 3:4–9

Truth Application

Are you active in Bible class or Sunday school? If not, enroll with an attitude to come prepared and to humbly participate.

Truth 50

I Don't Have to Help God Out

*I will wait patiently for God and not
rush to try and help Him out.*

Have you ever waited on someone, and it seemed as if they would never show up? What about the final hours or seconds before a deadline, and the person who promised to be there had not come through? Those are difficult and frustrating times. Well think about Joseph, Mary's husband. The Bible lets us know that he was a just man (Matthew 1:19). He no doubt studied Old Testament writings and like most devote Jewish men, eagerly awaited the birth of the Messiah. When an angel of the Lord appeared to him proclaiming that Mary was carrying the Messiah, Joseph's joy may have been tempered by prophesy which declared, the Messiah was to be born in Bethlehem. Yet Joseph lived in Nazareth (Micah 5:2). Joseph may have been tempted to go to Bethlehem to try to fulfill the prophecy. Fortunately, he waited and allowed God to move. When the decree went out from Rome to tax the world, Joseph by law was compelled to go back to his birthplace—Bethlehem (Luke 2:1–5). Although Mary was in the final stages of pregnancy, their hearts must have been encouraged and strengthened by the fact that God was fulfilling His Word. You'll value God's promises more if you allow Him to fulfill them. Wait patiently on God. The outcome will be encouraging, and He alone will get the glory. You don't have to help God out.

Scriptural Meditation
Luke 2:1–7, Psalms 27:13–14, and Matthew 2:1–15

Truth Application
When waiting on the Lord to fulfill His word, keep praises on your lips and sing to yourself in songs and hymns. Keep the Scriptures and Christian reading material on hand and always a notepad for jotting down ideas. You'll be able to redeem the time as you wait.

Truth 51

I Bury My Past

I am a new creation. My past is buried under the blood of Jesus and will not haunt me.

Praise God, your past isn't held against you. When you repent, your sins are removed as far from you as the east is from the west, and Jesus remembers them no more (Psalms 103:12 and Isaiah 43:25). If only we could do the same. We cannot live in the past or allow others to drag us back into bondage. From the moment you repent, go forward leaving the past just there—in the past. The Bible tells us about Rahab the prostitute (Joshua 2). When Israel crossed over into the land God had promised, Joshua sent out spies to scout the city of Jericho. The two spies entered Rahab's house and used it as a lookout. Rahab had heard how God destroyed cities for Israel and was convinced that Jericho would suffer the same fate. By faith, she asked to be saved from Jericho's destruction and was given a promise that when Israel overtook Jericho all those who choose to seek refuge inside her house would be saved. Joshua kept that promise, and Rahab and all her house were saved. She was integrated into the Hebrew community. In Matthew's genealogy of Jesus, Rahab is listed as the mother of Boaz, the great grandfather of King David (Matthew 1:5). Praise God, Rahab's past wasn't held against her. Once you become a part of the family of God, your past need not haunt you. Bury your past and go forward in Christ.

Scriptural Meditation

Philippians 3:13–14, II Corinthians 5:17, Joshua 2:1–14 and 6:22–25

Truth Application

If you are haunted by your past, pray a prayer of repentance, accept forgiveness, and then have a guilt and shame burying ceremony. Write down things God has cleansed you from on a piece of paper then tear it up and throw it away. Let this ritual symbolize a fresh start.

Truth 52

I Am Because God Is

I am made in God's image. As He fought fleshy, carnal feelings, so will I.

Thank God we have a savior who is touched with the feelings of our infirmities. Who was tempted as we are yet didn't sin (Hebrews 4:15). It makes a difference that Jesus understood the frailties of humanity. He cried, was sorrowful, felt rejection and loneliness. Although he was God, he constrained himself to a physical body and walked this earth as the Son. Not yielding to his will but to that of the Father. He is our example. We don't have to allow our emotions and our frailties to be our shortcoming. The fact that we are made in the image of God is an asset given to us by God that elevates us above all of creation. What a blessing! The next time you feel your emotions pulling you down to a mere carnal level, lift your eyes and heart toward the Lord knowing that God designed you to walk in the fullness of the Spirit, not relish in the dysfunctionalities of the flesh. We have to know that since Jesus suffered being tempted in the flesh, he is able to help those who are being tempted. Your source for victorious living is found in your ability to believe and receive from Christ. You can do all things through Christ who strengthens you.

Scriptural Meditation
Genesis 1:26–31, Hebrews 2, Romans 8

Truth Application
When you're struggling emotionally, feeling rejected, sorrowful or lonely, commit to pronouncing aloud and repeatedly Philippians 4:13, "I can do all things through Christ who strengthens me," as a remedy, pulling yourself out of human frailty and into the power of the spirit.

About the Author

Myrna R. Herndon is a lifelong learner who enjoys Bible study, history and current affairs. She is a licensed Missionary/Evangelist with the Church of God in Christ Inc. and a graduate of the DeVos Urban Leadership Initiative. Missionary Herndon is a Bible teacher, conference speaker and women's ministry leader in both her international denomination and local church, Hallelujah Temple in Park Forest, Illinois. She holds a Bachelor of Science degree in radio, TV and film from Northwestern University in Evanston, Illinois, and has over thirty years of experience as a producer/writer in corporate and broadcast production. She is a mentor to youth and new Christian converts, utilizing creative arts to build positive esteem while cultivating spiritual growth. Missionary Herndon resides in Flossmoor, Illinois, with her loving husband of nearly forty years, Pastor Dr. Astead N. Herndon. They are the proud parents of three adult children. She enjoys spending time with family, reading, traveling, puzzles, and attending the theater. For more information, visit www.myrnaherndon.com.

Ophelia Davis
708 248-0114

CPSIA information can be obtained
at www.ICGtesting.com
Printed in the USA
FFHW021901200719
53736542-59434FF